Creative Frittata

Cookbook

Creative & Delicious Fritta

Breakfast, Lunch or

BY

Stephanie Sharp

License Notes

My deepest thanks for buying my book! Now that you have made this investment in time and money, you are now eligible for free e-books on a weekly basis! Once you subscribe by filling in the box below with your email address, you will start to receive free and discounted book offers for unique and informative books. There is nothing more to do! A reminder email will be sent to you a few days before the promotion expires so you will never have to worry about missing out on this amazing deal. Enter your email address below to get started. Thanks again for your purchase!

Just visit the link or scan QR-code to get started!

https://stephanie-sharp.subscribemenow.com

Table of Contents

wwwwwwwwwwwwwwwwwwwwwwwwwwwww

Introduction

Welcome to our journey through the world of frittatas. Frittatas are one of the hidden delights of simple and can be enjoyed as so much more than breakfast. That is exactly why this Creative Frittata Cookbook was created.

This Cookbook will introduce you to 30delicious frittata recipes that are so easy that you can enjoy doing them with the whole family. Best of all, the frittata recipes featured are all simple to make, tasty and incredibly filling.

All you need to do to get started is flip the page and head to the kitchen. Are you ready to dive into this frittata journey? Let's do it!

Mushroom Frittata

This delicious frittata is earthy and filling.

Serving Size: 6

Cooking Time: 10 mins

Ingredients:

- 1 tbsp butter or margarine
- 1 C. sliced mushrooms
- 1/2 C. chopped green and/or red peppers
- 1/3 C. chopped onion
- 12 eggs
- 1/4 C. water

Directions:

1. Place a large skillet over medium heat. Add the butter and cook it until it melts completely. Cook in it the onion with peppers and mushroom for 6 min.

2. Get a large mixing bowl: Add the eggs with water and whisk them well. Spread the mix all over the cooked veggies.

3. Put on the lid and cook them until its bottom is set. Flip the Frittata and cook it until it set on the other side.

4. Flip your Frittata back and broil it in the oven for 2 min. Serve it warm with your favorite toppings.

5. Enjoy.

The Pepper Jack Pepper Frittata

If you love pepper jack cheese then you.

Serving Size: 8

Cooking Time: 40 mins

Ingredients:

- 8 eggs
- 2 tbsp. water
- 1 C. shredded pepper jack cheese, divided
- 1/2 C. fresh tarragon
- 1/2 C. minced red bell pepper
- 1/2 tsp fresh ground black pepper

Directions:

1. Set your oven to 350 degrees before doing anything else.

2. Get a bowl, combine: water and eggs.

3. Stir the mix until it is smooth then add in half a C. of cheese, tarragon, black pepper, and bell peppers.

4. Stir the mix until it is smooth then top it with the rest of the cheese.

5. Enter everything into a pie dish then cook the frittata in the oven for 35 mins.

6. Enjoy.

Feta Frittata

This Feta Frittata is easy to whip up and tasty.

Serving Size: 4

Cooking Time: 35 mins

Ingredients:

- 2 tbsp olive oil
- 1/2 C. red bell pepper, cut into thin matchsticks
- 1/2 C. chopped onion
- 3 eggs
- 1/2 C. milk
- 1 (10 oz) package frozen chopped spinach, thawed and squeezed dry
- 1 C. chopped cooked ham
- 1/2 C. shredded mozzarella cheese
- 1/2 C. crumbled feta cheese
- 1/2 tsp salt
- 1/4 tsp ground black pepper

Directions:

1. Place a large pan over medium heat. Add the olive oil and heat it. Cook in it the onion with pepper for 6 min.

2. Get a large mixing bowl: Whisk in it the milk with eggs. Stir in the spinach, cooked onion, ham, mozzarella cheese, feta cheese, salt, and black pepper.

3. Pour the mix back into the pan and put on the lid. Cook the Frittata for 9 min. Serve your Frittata warm with your favorite toppings.

4. Enjoy.

wwwwwwwwwwwwwwwwwwwwwwwwwwwwwwww

The Garden Frittata

This Garden Frittata is both healthy and delish.

Serving Size: 4

Cooking Time: 15 mins

Ingredients:

- 4 small yellow squash
- 1 tbsp butter
- 6 eggs
- 1/2 C. cheddar cheese, shredded
- 1 tsp Italian seasoning
- 1/4 tsp salt
- 1/2 tsp pepper

Directions:

1. Cut your squash into thin slices. Then fry them in butter until crispy.

2. Get a bowl, combine: pepper, eggs, salt, Italian seasoning, and shredded cheese.

3. Add the egg mix to the squash in the pan and let the mix cook for 10 mins with a low level of heat and a lid on the pot.

4. Now place the frittata under the broiler for 3 mins to cook the top.

5. Enjoy.

wwwwwwwwwwwwwwwwwwwwwwwwwwwwwwwwww

Button Cheddar Frittata

This is a fun recipe to do with the whole family.

Serving Size: 4

Cooking Time: 40 mins

Ingredients:

- 1 serving cooking spray (optional)
- 1 tbsp olive oil, or as needed
- 1/2 onion, chopped
- 1/2 red bell pepper, diced
- 4 button mushrooms, diced
- 1 stalk fresh asparagus, trimmed and chopped
- 6 egg whites
- 2 eggs
- 1/3 C. skim milk
- 1 C. shredded Cheddar cheese

Directions:

1. Before you do anything preheat the oven to 375 F. Coat a casserole dish with a cooking spray.

2. Place a large pan over medium heat. Add the olive oil and heat it. Cook in it the onion, red bell pepper, mushrooms, and asparagus for 8 min.

3. Place the mix in the casserole dish and spread it.

4. Get a large mixing bowl: Add the egg whites, eggs, and skim milk. Whisk them well. Pour the mix all over the cooked veggies mix.

5. Cook the Frittata in the oven for 24 min. Serve it warm.

6. Enjoy.

wwwwwwwwwwwwwwwwwwwwwwwwwwwwwwwwwww

Fontina and Sun-Dried Frittata

Here is a recipe that can be enjoyed as any course in the day.

Serving Size: 4

Cooking Time: 20 mins

Ingredients:

- 8 oz. spaghetti
- 1/2 C. sun-dried tomato packed in oil, drained and chopped
- 4 large eggs
- 1 1/2 tsps. salt
- 1/2 tsp ground black pepper
- 3/4 C. parmesan cheese, shredded
- 3/4 C. Fontina cheese, shredded
- 1 tbsp butter
- 1 tbsp extra virgin olive oil

Directions:

1. Boil your spaghetti in water and salt for 9 mins then remove the liquids and combine the pasta with the sun-dried tomatoes.

2. Get a bowl and combine fontina, eggs, parmesan, pepper, and salt.

3. Stir the mix until it is smooth then stir in the eggs.

4. Place the mix into a large frying pan with hot butter and cook the mix for 4 mins with a medium level of heat.

5. Now put everything under the broiler for 6 mins.

6. Enjoy.

wwwwwwwwwwwwwwwwwwwwwwwwwwwwww

Saltine Artichoke Hearts Frittata

If you like artichokes, you will love this frittata.

Serving Size: 12

Cooking Time: 1 hr

Ingredients:

- artichoke hearts, chopped, 12 oz., marinated, drained (marinade reserved)
- green onions, 1 bunch, chopped
- eggs, 9, beaten
- Cheddar cheese, 1 lb., sharp, grated
- saltine crackers, 14, crumbled
- parsley, 1/2 C., chopped
- garlic, 2 cloves, minced
- hot pepper sauce, 1 dash
- salt and black pepper, to taste

Directions:

1. Before you do anything preheat the oven to 325 F. Coat a casserole dish with a cooking spray.

2. Place a large pan over medium heat. Pour in it 3 tbsp of the artichoke marinade and heat it. Add the green onion and cook it for 4 min.

3. Get a large mixing bowl: Stir in it the cooked pepper, salt, hot sauce, garlic, parsley, saltine crackers, cheddar, eggs and green onions.

4. Pour the mix into the greased casserole. Place it in the oven and cook it for 42 min. Serve your Frittata warm with your favorite toppings.

5. Enjoy.

wwwwwwwwwwwwwwwwwwwwwwwwwwwwwwwwwww

Italian Pasta Frittata

That's right this frittata will remind you of a bowl of Italian pasta.

Serving Size: 2

Cooking Time: 17 mins

Ingredients:

- 6 oz. cooked pasta, coated with tomato sauce
- 4 eggs
- 2 oz. shredded parmesan cheese
- 3 oz. butter
- salt & freshly ground black pepper

Directions:

1. Get a bowl combine: cheese, eggs, and pasta.

2. Stir the mix then add in some pepper and salt.

3. Melt 1/2 of your butter in a frying pan then add the pasta mix, set the heat to low, and let everything cook for 12 mins.

4. Invert the pan over a plate then place the opposite side of the frittata facing downwards in the pan.

5. Continue frying everything for 4 more mins.

6. Enjoy.

Charlottesville Potato Frittata

If you are from the south, then this frittata is for you.

Serving Size: 8

Cooking Time: 45 mins.

Ingredients:

- 1 (9.6 oz) package Sausage Crumbles
- 2 C. cubed cooked red potatoes
- 8 eggs
- 1/4 C. grated Parmesan cheese
- 1/4 tsp salt
- 1/4 tsp ground black pepper
- 1/2 C. chopped seeded tomato
- 2 green onions, thinly sliced

Directions:

1. Place a large pan over medium heat. Add the sausages and brown them for 6 min. Add the potato and spread them in the pan.

2. Get a large mixing bowl: Whisk in it the eggs, cheese, salt and pepper. Spread the mix over the sausage and potato mix.

3. Increase the heat to medium high and cook them for 3 min wile titling the pan to fill the edges with uncooked eggs mix.

4. Lower the heat to medium low and put on the lid. Cook them for 16 min. Serve your Frittata with onion and potato.

5. Enjoy.

wwwwwwwwwwwwwwwwwwwwwwwwwwwwwww

Dijon and Cheddar Frittata

This delicious frittata is cheesy, tasty and easy to make.

Serving Size: 4

Cooking Time: 25 mins

Ingredients:

- 6 slices bacon
- 7 eggs
- 1/4 C. milk
- 1 tsp Dijon mustard
- 1 C. coarsely chopped seeded tomatoes
- 1 garlic clove, minced
- 1 C. shredded cheddar cheese

Directions:

1. Fry your bacon until fully done then place the bacon to the side and crumble it.

2. Keep about 2 tbsp of fat in the pan and begin to stir fry your garlic and tomatoes for 4 mins then add the bacon.

3. At the same time get a bowl, combine: mustard, milk, and eggs.

4. Add the egg mix to the tomato mix and set the heat to low.

5. Let the frittata cook for 5 mins until the bottom is fully set then top everything with the cheese and place a lid on the pan.

6. Shut the heat and let the frittata sit until the cheese is melted for about 5 mins.

7. Enjoy.

Cheesy Italian Hearts Frittata

Here is yet another delicious artichoke recipe.

Serving Size: 6

Cooking Time: 50 mins

Ingredients:

- Salami, 1/2 C., diced
- artichoke hearts, 1/2 C., chopped, drained
- cherry tomatoes, 1/2 C., chopped
- mushrooms, 4.5oz., sliced, drained
- eggs, 6
- milk, 1/3 C.
- green onions, 2, chopped
- garlic, 1 clove, minced
- basil, 1 tsp., dried
- onion powder, 1 tsp.
- salt, 1 tsp.
- black pepper, to taste
- Parmesan cheese, 1/3 C., grated
- mozzarella cheese, 1 C., shredded

Directions:

1. Before you do anything preheat the oven to 425 F. Coat a casserole dish with a cooking spray.

2. Place a large pan over medium heat. Grease it with some oil. Add the mushrooms, tomatoes, artichokes and salami.

3. Cook them for 5 min. Spread the mix in the casserole dish.

4. Get a large mixing bowl: Combine in it the pepper, salt, onion powder, basil, garlic, green onions, milk and eggs. Mix them well.

5. Pour the mix all over the cooked veggies mix. Top them with parmesan and mozzarella cheese. Cook them in the oven for 22 min.

6. Serve your cheesy frittata warm.

7. Enjoy.

wwwwwwwwwwwwwwwwwwwwwwwwwwwwwww

Country Side Frittata

Yet another southern recipe that your whole family will love.

Serving Size: 21

Cooking Time: 15 mins.

Ingredients:

- Milk, 2 tbsp.
- Eggs, 2
- Parsley, 1 tbsp., chopped
- Garlic, 1 clove, crushed
- chili pepper flakes, 1 pinch, dried
- white bread, 1 slice, torn into small pieces
- sea salt & ground pepper
- olive oil, 1 tbsp.
- parmesan cheese, 1 tbsp., shredded

Directions:

1. Get a bowl, combine: garlic, pepper flakes, parsley, bread, eggs and milk.

2. Let the bread sit submerged in the mix until everything is absorbed.

3. Now add the egg mix to the skillet with hot oil and cook everything for 5 mins.

4. Invert the pan on a plate and place the opposite side of the frittata in the pan.

5. Top everything with parmesan and cook the contents for 3 more mins until the bottom is set and cheese melts.

6. Enjoy.

Muffin Frittata

This delicious Muffin Frittata is the perfect breakfast meal.

Serving Size: 12

Cooking Time: 45 mins.

Ingredients:

- 1 C. zucchini, shredded
- 1/2 C. red pepper, minced
- 2 garlic cloves, minced
- 1 tbsp margarine or 1 tbsp butter
- 1 C. cooked rice
- 1/2 C. part-skim mozzarella cheese, shredded
- 3 eggs, beaten
- 1/2 C. skim milk
- 1 1/4 tsps. dried Italian seasoning
- 1/2 tsp salt
- cooking spray

Directions:

1. Stir fry your garlic, pepper, and zucchini in margarine with a medium level of heat then remove any liquids and add in the rice.

2. Let the mix cool then combine in the cheese.

3. Set your oven to 350 degrees before doing anything else.

4. Add 1 tbsp of rice mix into the sections of a mini muffin pan after coating the pan with nonstick spray.

5. Get a bowl, combine: salt, eggs, Italian seasoning, and milk.

6. Stir the mix until it is smooth then evenly divide everything between the muffin sections.

7. Cook the frittata for 30 mins in the oven then let it sit for 10 mins.

8. Enjoy.

The Latin Frittata

If Mexican cuisine is your preference this recipe will be definitely a go.

Serving Size: 6

Cooking Time: 40 mins.

Ingredients:

- 1 tbsp olive oil
- 1 small onion, minced
- 3/4 lb. chorizo sausage, chopped
- 6 oz. frozen tater tots, thawed
- 2 fresh garlic cloves, minced
- 1 C. roasted red pepper, chopped
- 12 large eggs, beaten
- 1 C. Monterey Jack cheese, shredded
- 1 large avocado, sliced
- 1/8 C. sour cream
- 1/8 C. salsa
- 3 tbsp. scallions, finely sliced
- 3 sprigs cilantro leaves, for garnish

Directions:

1. Add your tater tots to a bowl and mash them evenly.

2. Combine your chorizo and onions in olive oil and stir fry them for 7 mins.

3. Then add in the tater tots, red pepper, and garlic.

4. Cook everything until the potatoes hot. Then add in the egg mix and combine everything evenly.

5. Set the heat to low and place a lid on the pan.

6. Cook the frittata until the bottom has set then place everything under the broiler for 3 mins.

7. Top the frittata with the cheese and let it sit in the pan with the lid placed on it.

8. Top everything with the cilantro, scallions, salsa, and avocado.

9. Enjoy.

Healthy Frittata

This frittata will be done in a flash.

Serving Size: 4

Cooking Time: 35 mins.

Ingredients:

- 1 C. egg substitute
- 1/4 C. nonfat milk
- 1 tbsp fresh dill, chopped
- 3/4 tsp salt
- 1/4 tsp ground pepper
- 1/2 lb. fresh white mushroom, sliced
- 1 (15 oz.) cans white potatoes, drained and sliced
- 1 small red pepper, seeded and minced
- 1/2 C. onion, minced
- 1 (8 oz.) salmon fillets, skin removed, cut into 1-inch pieces

Directions:

1. Get your oven's broiler hot before doing anything else.

2. Get a bowl, combine: pepper, egg substitute, salt, milk, and dill.

3. Coat a frying pan with nonstick spray then begin to fry your mushrooms for 7 mins.

4. Combine in the onion, red pepper, and potatoes.

5. Cook the mix for 4 mins.

6. Now add in the salmon and cook the fish for 4 mins.

7. Top everything with the egg mix and set the heat to low.

8. Place a lid on the pot and let the frittata cook for 8 mins.

9. Now cook the frittata for 4 mins under the broiler.

10. Enjoy.

wwwwwwwwwwwwwwwwwwwwwwwwwwwwwwww

Pesto Frittata

This Pesto Frittata is simple to whip up and very flavorful.

Serving Size: 4

Cooking Time: 30 mins

Ingredients:

- 1 tbsp oil
- 6 medium onions, sliced
- 1 tsp brown sugar
- 4 garlic cloves, chopped
- 8 eggs, beaten
- 3/4 C. milk
- 1/4 C. pesto sauce,
- 3/4 C. shredded cheddar cheese
- salt, to taste
- fresh ground black pepper, to taste

Directions:

1. Get a bowl combine: pesto, milk, and eggs.

2. Begin to stir fry your onions after topping them with sugar, in oil, for 15 mins.

3. Combine in the garlic when 5 more mins of cooking time is left.

4. Now add in your eggs and let the bottom set for 7 mins.

5. Top the frittata with the cheese and some pepper and salt.

6. Now place the frittata under the broiler for 4 mins.

7. Enjoy.

wwwwwwwwwwwwwwwwwwwwwwwwwwwwwwwww

Jalapeno Frittata

This frittata is spicy yet simply delicious.

Serving Size: 4

Cooking Time: 44 mins

Ingredients:

- 1 tbsp olive oil
- 1/2 C. cooked ham, cubed
- 1/2 C. onion, chopped
- 1/4 C. red sweet bell pepper, chopped
- 1/4 C. green bell pepper, chopped
- 1/4 C. celery, chopped
- 2 jalapeno peppers, seeded and chopped
- 2 tbsp. jalapeno jelly, at room temperature
- 6 eggs, beaten
- 1/4 tsp salt
- 1/2 tsp cracked black pepper or 1/2 tsp red pepper flakes
- 1/4 C. cheddar cheese, shredded

Directions:

1. Set your oven to 400 degrees before doing anything else.

2. Begin to stir fry your onions and ham in oil for 8 mins then combine in the jalapeno jelly, bell peppers, celery, and jalapeno peppers.

3. Continue frying the mix for 4 mins.

4. Get a bowl, combine: pepper, salt, and eggs.

5. Add the eggs to the pepper mix and let the bottom of the frittata set with a lid place on the pan.

6. Once the bottom has set place the frittata in the oven for 22 mins until it is fully done. Then top everything with the cheddar and place it under the broiler for 4 mins.

7. Enjoy.

wwwwwwwwwwwwwwwwwwwwwwwwwwwwwwwwww

Dijon and Pepper Frittata

This delicious frittata is smooth in texture and spicy in flavor.

Serving Size: 4

Cooking Time: 37 mins

Ingredients:

- 5 eggs
- 1/2 C. milk or 1/2 C. half-and-half cream
- 1 tbsp Dijon mustard
- 1 C. crouton
- 1/4 C. ham, chopped
- 1/2 C. fontina or 1/2 C. provolone cheese, shredded
- 1/4 C. roasted red pepper, drained and chopped
- 1/4 C. green onion, minced, greens

Directions:

1. Set your oven to 350 degrees before doing anything else.

2. Get a bowl and beat your eggs in it, then add in the Dijon and milk.

3. Continue to whisk the mix then add half of the cheese, half of the green onions, half of the bell peppers, the croutons and the ham.

4. Stir the mix then pour everything into a pie dish coated with nonstick spray.

5. Top everything with the rest of the green onions, bell pepper, and cheese.

6. Cook the frittata in the oven for 25 mins then let it sit for 10 mins.

7. Enjoy.

wwwwwwwwwwwwwwwwwwwwwwwwwwwwwwwwww

Spicy Buttery Frittata

The butter in this recipe helps to make for a smooth and spicy bite.

Serving Size: 6

Cooking Time: 20 mins

Ingredients:

- 60 g butter
- 4 large thinly sliced onions
- 6 eggs
- 2 garlic cloves, crushed
- salt & ground black pepper
- 1 chili, minced

Directions:

1. Stir fry your onions, chili, and garlic in butter.

2. Get a bowl combine pepper, salt, and eggs.

3. Remove the onions from the pan then add in more butter and also add in the eggs and then onions.

4. Cook the frittata until the bottom sets then flip it and cook the opposite side.

5. Enjoy.

Peas and Parmesan Frittata

This tasty frittata is both filling and easy to make.

Serving Size: 4

Cooking Time: 40 mins.

Ingredients:

- 6 eggs
- 1/2 C. evaporated low-fat milk
- 20 g butter
- 1 medium leek, thinly sliced
- 2/3 C. frozen peas
- 2 medium tomatoes, thinly sliced
- 2 tbsps. finely shredded parmesan cheese
- salt
- pepper

Directions:

1. Get a bowl combine evaporated milk and eggs.

2. Stir the mix until it is smooth then add in the pepper and salt.

3. Begin to stir fry your leeks in butter until they are soft.

4. Then turn on your broiler.

5. Add the tomato and peas to the pan then add the eggs.

6. Set the heat to low and let the bottom of the eggs set.

7. Once the bottom has set top everything with parmesan and place the frittata under the broiler and for 4 mins.

8. Enjoy.

wwwwwwwwwwwwwwwwwwwwwwwwwwwwwwwww

Artisan Frittata

This delicious frittata takes you to heaven and back with every sophisticated bite.

Serving Size: 4

Cooking Time: 25 mins.

Ingredients:

- 9 large eggs
- 1/4 C. freshly shredded parmesan cheese
- 4 oz. feta cheese, crumbled
- 2 tbsps. minced fresh dill
- kosher salt
- fresh ground black pepper
- 2 tbsps. olive oil
- 1 clove garlic, minced
- 4 C. packed arugula, stemmed, washed and dried

Directions:

1. Set your oven to 400 degrees before doing anything else.

2. Whisk your eggs then combine in the pepper, salt, dill, and cheeses.

3. Whisk the mix again then begin to fry your garlic in oil.

4. Once the garlic is browned add the arugula and continue frying everything for 3 mins, set the heat to low and spread out the arugula.

5. Pour in your eggs and let the bottom set for 2 mins then place everything in the oven for 13 mins.

6. Enjoy.

wwwwwwwwwwwwwwwwwwwwwwwwwwwwwwww

Classical Morning Frittata

If you love the traditional breakfast frittata then this delicious frittata will be perfect for you.

Serving Size: 6

Cooking Time: 30 mins.

Ingredients:

- 1 lb. Jimmy Dean sausage
- 6 eggs
- 3 C. potatoes, chopped
- 1/4 C. onion
- 2 tbsps. bell peppers, chopped
- 2 tbsps. sweet red peppers, chopped
- 4 oz. Monterey Jack pepper cheese, chopped
- 4 oz. sharp cheddar cheese, shredded
- 2 tsps. salt
- 2 tbsps. half-and-half
- 2 tsps. hot sauce
- 1/2 tsp baking soda
- 2 tsps. pepper
- 2 tbsps. olive oil

Directions:

1. Set your oven to 350 degrees before doing anything else.

2. Fry your sausages then place them to the side.

3. Now fry your potatoes until they are brown, in oil, in a frying pan, then combine in the chopped pepper and onions.

4. Cook the mix until the onions are see-through.

5. Get a bowl and whisk your eggs then add in the baking soda, hot sauce, and half and half.

6. Add the eggs to the sausage mix in the pan then add your pepper jack cheese after dicing it then top everything with pepper and salt.

7. Top the mix further with the shredded cheddar and let the bottom of the frittata set in the pan.

8. Now place everything into the oven for 15 mins.

9. Enjoy.

wwwwwwwwwwwwwwwwwwwwwwwwwwwwwww

Green Feta Frittata

This frittata is both healthy and delicious.

Serving Size: 6

Cooking Time: 30 mins.

Ingredients:

- 1 (9 oz.) bags Baby Spinach
- 1 tbsp. olive oil, divided
- 2 tsps. olive oil, divided
- 1 C. yellow onion, chopped
- 6 large eggs
- 1/2 C. sun-dried tomato packed in oil, drained
- 1/2 C. feta cheese, crumbled
- 1 tsp. dried Italian seasoning
- 1/4 tsp. salt
- 1/8 tsp. black pepper

Directions:

1. Get your oven's broiler hot then add your spinach to a bowl. Cook the spinach in the microwave for 4 mins with the highest level of heat.

2. At the same time coat a frying pan with cooking spray then add in 1 tbsp of oil and begin to fry your onions until browned.

3. Get a bowl, combine: eggs, pepper, tomatoes, salt, spinach, Italian seasoning, and cheese.

4. Pour everything into the onions and cook them for 6 mins until the bottom is set.

5. Now place the frittata under the broiler for 3 mins.

6. Enjoy.

wwwwwwwwwwwwwwwwwwwwwwwwwwwwwwwww

Tomato and Potato Frittata

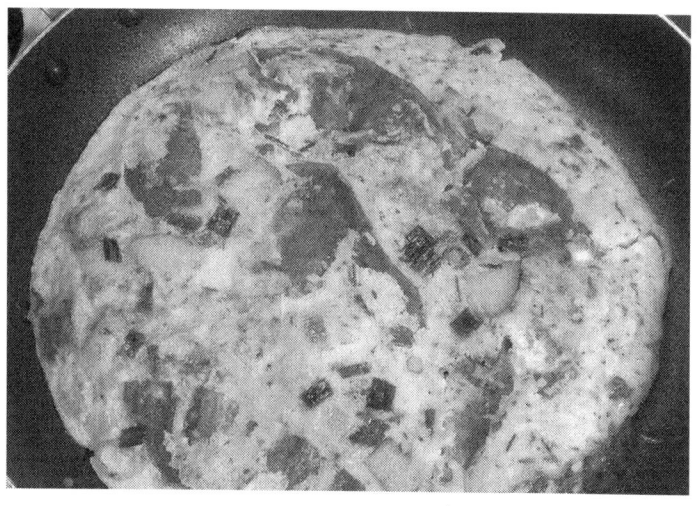

For a lunch time or dinner frittata try this delicious frittata.

Serving Size: 8

Cooking Time: 45 mins

Ingredients:

- pork sausage, 10oz., crumbles
- red potatoes, 2 C., cubed and cooked
- eggs, 8
- parmesan cheese, 1/4 C., shredded
- salt, 1/4 tsp.
- black pepper, 1/4 tsp., ground
- tomatoes, 1/2 C., seeded and chopped
- green onions, 2 stalks, thinly sliced

Directions:

1. For 5 mins stir fry your sausage then combine in the potatoes.

2. Get a bowl, combine: pepper, eggs, salt, and cheese.

3. Beat the mix until it is smooth then add everything to the potatoes.

4. Let the mix cook for 3 mins with a high level of heat then set the heat to low and place a lid on the pot.

5. Let the frittata cook for 15 mins then add a topping of onions and tomatoes.

6. Enjoy.

wwwwwwwwwwwwwwwwwwwwwwwwwwwwwww

Curds and Chili Frittata

This delicious Chili and Curds Frittata can be whipped up in minutes and enjoyed for any course of the day.

Serving Size: 8

Cooking Time: 1 hr.

Ingredients:

- Flour, 1/2 C.
- baking powder, 1 tsp.
- eggs, 10, lightly beaten
- butter, 1/4 lb., melted and slightly cooled
- Monterey Jack cheese, 1 lb., shredded
- green chilies, 12oz., chopped, canned
- curd cottage cheese, 2 C.
- salt, to taste

Directions:

1. Set your oven to 350 degrees before doing anything else.

2. Coat a casserole dish with butter then combine your baking powder and flour in bowl.

3. Add in the butter and the eggs as well and mix everything well.

4. Now add the rest of the ingredients then place everything into the casserole dish.

5. Cook the frittata in the oven for 40 mins.

6. Enjoy.

Andouille Frittata

This exotic frittata is delicious and simple to make.

Serving Size: 4

Cooking Time: 38 mins.

Ingredients:

- 1 tbsp butter
- 1/4 C. sliced green onion
- 4 oz. medium mushrooms, sliced
- 3 oz. andouille sausages, sliced in half lengthwise and cut into 1/8-inch pieces
- 6 large eggs
- 2 tbsps. milk or water
- 1 1/2 C. cheddar cheese, divided
- 1/4 C. chopped parsley
- salt and pepper

Directions:

1. Stir fry your sausages, mushrooms, and green onions in butter for 12 mins.

2. Get a bowl, combine: some pepper, eggs, some salt, milk, parsley, and 2 C. of cheese.

3. Add the eggs to the sausages in the pan and set the heat to low.

4. Place a lid on the pot and cook everything for 11 mins. Top the frittata with cheese and place it all in the broiler for 2 mins.

5. Enjoy.

wwwwwwwwwwwwwwwwwwwwwwwwwwwwww

Simple Italian Frittata

If you love Italian cuisine this frittata will quickly become your favorite dish.

Serving Size: 4

Cooking Time: 35 mins.

Ingredients:

- 1 C. thinly sliced onion
- 1 tsp olive oil
- 1 medium tomatoes, chopped
- salt and pepper
- 1/4 C. fresh basil, chopped
- 4 tbsps. parmesan cheese
- 4 eggs
- 1 tbsp water

Directions:

1. Stir fry your onions until see through, in oil, then combine in the pepper, salt, and tomatoes.

2. Cook everything for 7 mins.

3. Combine in the basil and stir the mix.

4. Let the spices cook for 3 mins then remove everything from the pan.

5. Coat the pan with nonstick spray.

6. Now combine 3 tbsp of parmesan with the eggs, and water until foamy then add the eggs to the pan.

7. Set the heat to low and let the frittata cook for 12 mins then place everything under the broiler after topping it with the rest of the parmesan for 3 mins.

8. Enjoy.

wwwwwwwwwwwwwwwwwwwwwwwwwwwwwwww

Broccoli & Ham Frittata

This Ham and Broccoli Frittata will keep you full for hours with a delicious taste in your mouth.

Serving Size: 6

Cooking Time: 1 hr.

Ingredients:

- 1 C. broccoli floret
- 3/4 C. sliced fresh mushrooms
- 2 green onions, minced
- 1 tbsp butter
- 1 C. cooked ham, cubed
- 8 eggs
- 1/4 C. water
- 1/4 C. Dijon mustard
- 1/2 tsp Italian seasoning
- 1/4 tsp garlic salt
- 1 1/2 C. cheddar cheese, shredded (6 oz.)
- 1/2 C. tomatoes, chopped

Directions:

1. Stir fry your onion, mushrooms, and broccoli until it is soft, in butter. Then remove everything from the pan.

2. Get a bowl combine: garlic salt, eggs, Italian seasoning, water, and mustard.

3. Now set your oven to 375 degrees before doing anything else.

4. Stir the mix until it is smooth then add in the broccoli mix, tomatoes, and cheese.

5. Place everything into a casserole dish coated with nonstick spray and cook it all in the oven for 25 mins.

6. Enjoy.

wwwwwwwwwwwwwwwwwwwwwwwwwwwwww

Seafood Frittata

This delicious frittata is perfect for both pescatarians and seafood lovers alike.

Serving Size: 2

Cooking Time: 21 mins

Ingredients:

- 6 large eggs
- 3 tbsps. milk
- 2 tbsps. olive oil
- 2 scallions, thinly sliced
- 3/4 lb. small shrimp, peeled and deveined
- 1 tsp dried thyme
- 1 tbsp chopped fresh parsley
- 1/2 tsp dried oregano
- salt and pepper

Directions:

1. Get a bowl and combine your milk and eggs.

2. Begin to stir fry your scallions for 2 mins in oil then add in the pepper, salt, shrimp, oregano, thyme, and parsley.

3. Stir the mix and cook everything until the shrimp are done.

4. Set the heat to low then add in your eggs.

5. Place a lid on the pot, and let the frittata cook for 10 mins then shut the heat and let it sit for 10 more mins.

6. Enjoy.

wwwwwwwwwwwwwwwwwwwwwwwwwwwwwww

Pine Nuts and Pesto Frittata

This delicious frittata is crunchy and flavorful.

Serving Size: 4

Cooking Time: 35 mins

Ingredients:

- 10 eggs
- 1 C. ricotta cheese
- 1 large onion, finely sliced
- 2 garlic cloves, minced
- 1/3 C. pine nuts
- 2 tbsps. olive oil
- 1 C. fresh basil, roughly minced
- 1 C. Parmigiano-Reggiano cheese, shredded
- salt and pepper

Directions:

1. Set your oven to 425 degrees before doing anything else.

2. Get a bowl combine: ricotta and eggs.

3. Beat the mix until it is smooth, add in your pepper and salt, and continue to whisk.

4. Begin to stir fry your pine nuts, garlic, and onions for 5 mins in oil then add the egg mix and cook it for 1 min.

5. Now top the frittata with Parmigiano and basil and cook it in the oven for 8 mins.

6. After 8 mins place the frittata under the broiler for 4 mins.

7. Enjoy.

wwwwwwwwwwwwwwwwwwwwwwwwwwwwwwww

Rustic Frittata

If you are a lover of traditional homey cuisine then you must try this delicious frittata.

Serving Size: 4

Cooking Time: 30 mins

Ingredients:

- 6 eggs
- salt
- white pepper
- 1 C. ricotta cheese
- 1/4 C. freshly shredded parmesan cheese
- 1 1/2 tbsps. chopped marjoram
- 1 clove garlic, crushed
- 1 tbsp olive oil, mixed with
- 1 tsp melted butter

Directions:

1. Get your broiler hot before doing anything else.

2. Now get a bowl, combine: garlic, white pepper, eggs, marjoram, salt, and cheese.

3. Add your butter and oil to the pan and get everything hot.

4. Add in your egg mix and set the heat to low.

5. Let the eggs cook for 13 mins until the bottom sets then place the pan under the broiler for 3 more mins.

6. Enjoy.

Conclusion

Congrats on completing all 30 delicious Frittata Recipes! We hope you enjoyed all 30 recipes and that they were easy to whip up and tasty.

So, what happens next?

In order to become better at making frittatas you will have to practice. Be sure to keep cooking and enjoying all the delicious recipes featured in this Creative Frittata Cookbook. All of which will be easy to follow and can be created in a hassle-free environment. So, whenever you feel like you have mastered all the recipes in this book, grab another one of our books and let your culinary creativity run wild.

Remember, drop us a review if you loved what you read and until we meet again, keep on cooking delicious food.

wwwwwwwwwwwwwwwwwwwwwwwwwwwwwww

About the Author

Born in New Germantown, Pennsylvania, Stephanie Sharp received a Masters degree from Penn State in English Literature. Driven by her passion to create culinary masterpieces, she applied and was accepted to The International Culinary School of the Art Institute where she excelled in French cuisine. She has married her cooking skills with an aptitude for business by opening her own small cooking school where she teaches students of all ages.

Stephanie's talents extend to being an author as well and she has written over 400 e-books on the art of cooking and baking that include her most popular recipes.

Sharp has been fortunate enough to raise a family near her hometown in Pennsylvania where she, her husband and children live in a beautiful rustic house on an extensive piece of land. Her other passion is taking care of the furry members of her family which include 3 cats, 2 dogs and a potbelly pig named Wilbur.

Watch for more amazing books by Stephanie Sharp coming out in the next few months.

Author's Afterthoughts

I am truly grateful to you for taking the time to read my book. I cherish all of my readers! Thanks ever so much to each of my cherished readers for investing the time to read this book!

With so many options available to you, your choice to buy my book is an honour, so my heartfelt thanks at reading it from beginning to end!

I value your feedback, so please take a moment to submit an honest and open review on Amazon so I can get valuable insight into my readers' opinions and others can benefit from your experience.

Thank you for taking the time to review!

Stephanie Sharp

For announcements about new releases, please

follow my author page on Amazon.com!

(Look for the Follow Bottom under the photo)

You can find that at:

https://www.amazon.com/author/stephanie-sharp

*or Scan **QR-code** below.*

Printed in Great Britain
by Amazon